Drawing 3D

A Guide to Making Your Art Leap off the page

Brenda Clark

Copyright © 2017 by Brenda Clark

All rights reserved. No part of this publication may be reproduced, distributed, or transmitted in any form or by any means, including photocopying, recording, or other electronic or mechanical methods, without the prior written permission of the author, except in the case of brief quotations embodied in critical reviews and certain other noncommercial uses permitted by copyright law.

Table of Contents

Chapter 1 - In the Beginning … 6

Chapter 2 - Your Shopping List … 8

Chapter 3 – Shading … 12

Chapter 4 - Sphere … 16

Chapter 5 - The cube … 18

Chapter 6 – Tower … 21

Chapter 7 – Pipe … 25

Chapter 8 - Rain Cloud … 30

Chapter 9 - Ladder … 33

Chapter 10 – Crack … 38

Chapter 11 - Webbed Sphere … 42

Chapter 12 – Walls … 46

Conclusion … 51

You want to learn, but...

You can't seem to wrap your head around how to make the drawings look like they are popping off of the page. You've tried video tutorials, but have gotten frustrated having to constantly pause and draw the point back to where you need it to watch it again. Many of the books you've purchased seem to sip steps, leaving you scratching your head. This book has been formatted to help you at every step of the way and leave you making pictures that seem to pop off of the page. Every detail, trick, and piece of advice has been included to answer your questions as you go from lesson to lesson. By the time you are finished with the lessons in this book, you will have the knowledge to make your own 3D creations. What are you waiting for?

Are you ready?

Welcome to the world of 3D art. This book will walk you through every aspect of the art form and hopefully answer every question along the way. I will be your guide as you go from Chapter to Chapter, from lesson to lesson on your journey to drawing in 3D. This book will:

• Give you advice on your journey to drawing.

• Give you a list on the tools you will need to get started.

• Teach you how shading can provide the illusion of depth and 3D.

• Give you step-by-step instructions on how to draw each picture from beginning to end.

So, if you're ready to start on your journey to your new hobby and making your pictures pop out of the page, swipe your screen and let's get to it.

Chapter 1 - In the Beginning

Drawing can be fulfilling and rewarding, especially when you see the expressions on other people's faces when they look at your work. There are a few things you need to keep in mind:

1. With practice comes speed.
Don't expect to be lightning fast right from the start. New hobbies take time to master, and drawing is no different. As you get used to the technique, the speed will come.

2. Ignore the other people.
One of the worst things you can do is compare your work with what you see online. It took months and sometimes years for the people you see online to get that skilled at drawing what you see online. It's better to keep all of your work and compare your most recent work to the work you did first starting out. This will give you a better idea of how much you have progressed.

3. Don't spend your money on the best stuff.
When just starting out, don't reach deep into your wallet get the tools you need to get started on your new hobby. Find the best deals and try to use things you have around the house. If you decide you like your new hobby, you can upgrade to the more professional tools and equipment. It doesn't make sense to but top-dollar tools when starting a new hobby.

4. It supposed to be relaxing.
If you find yourself getting frustrated, take a break. It's new to you; so, don't expect to be an expert first starting out. If you need to walk away and take breaks, go ahead. Your new hobby is supposed to be relaxing, not taxing or stressful.

5. Find like minds online.
There are forums for everything online and art is not excluded. You will find art forums with people that give even more advice tips.

6. Don't stop with this book.
Take pictures of thing outside and even draw things in your room and try to draw them. Never stop practicing.

Chapter 2 - Your Shopping List

Every hobby needs tools in order to do it. Drawing is no different. Here is a list of things you will need to get started.

The Basics

Pencils

You will need either a no. 2 pencil or a mechanical pencil with HB or 2H lead to get started.

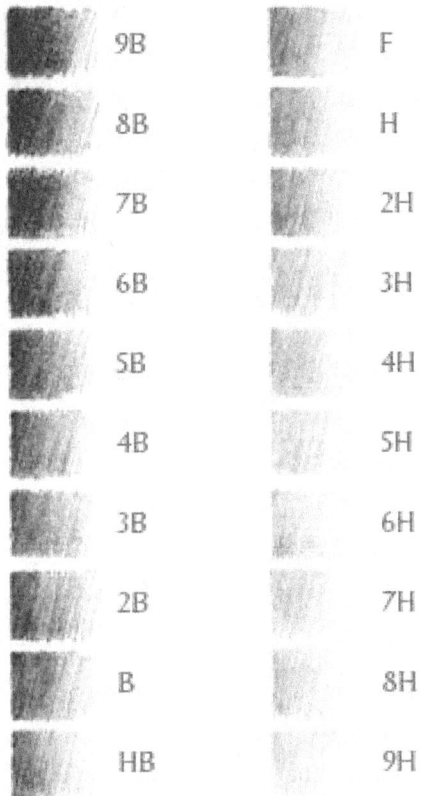

To the left, there is a chart. This chart shows you the different hardness levels the pencils can have when you find you like to draw and want to add more dimension to your work.

Erasers

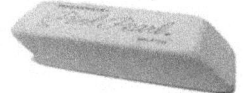

You can start out with a simple pink eraser. When you want to do more difficult art pieces, will also want a kneaded eraser. These can be used to smudge and lighten pencil marks.

Sketch Pad

You can start your new hobby using notebook paper, but sketch paper is recommended. There are different sizes of these pads, but the standard size is always the best to start out with.

Chair

This may not seem like it needs to be said, but you need a chair with lumbar support and that is comfortable enough to sit in for long periods of time.

Table/Desk

First starting out, using any table in the home is best as long as you don't have to either reach up to draw or bend over to draw because you are taller than your work space. A desk with a tilting surface is best when you're ready to upgrade.

Lighting

This is key. It isn't healthy to strain your eyes trying to see the finer details in your drawing pieces. Using a soft light that gives you true color is highly recommended. This will come in handy when you decide you are ready to start incorporating color into your artwork.

More advanced tools

When you find you are ready to continue your hobby, there will be a few extra things you will want to purchase.

Coloring tools

This can be charcoal, pastels, water colors, coloring pencils, and even art markers. You will have to experiment to find which medium you like best to add color to your art.

T-Square

This will help keep your lines straight and also help when you are using triangles, rulers and other tools.

Triangles

This will come in handy for more advanced drawings like buildings and vehicles. They can also be useful for straight lines.

Ruler

This can be added to the basic tools, too. If you need help with simple lines, rulers will do the trick.

Horse Hair Brush

This is helpful for sweeping the eraser shavings off of your drawings without smudging your drawing.

Eraser guard

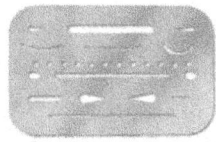

This is the perfect tool for erasing the lines you don't want while not touching the lines you want to keep.

Smudge Sticks/Blending Stumps

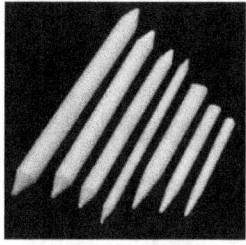

These come in all shapes and sizes and are designed to help you seamlessly blend shadows together to perfect shading.

Chapter 3 – Shading

You can't properly master 3D rendering without being able to grasp all the techniques for shading as they play a major role in creating the illusion of your picture leaping from the page. Above are the different ways you can add shading to your art pieces. Each has a different time and reason for use.

Hatching

This technique is used for basic shading and is used to cast shadows that are more linear.

Cross Hatching

This is the practice of hatching in two different directions to darken the shading.

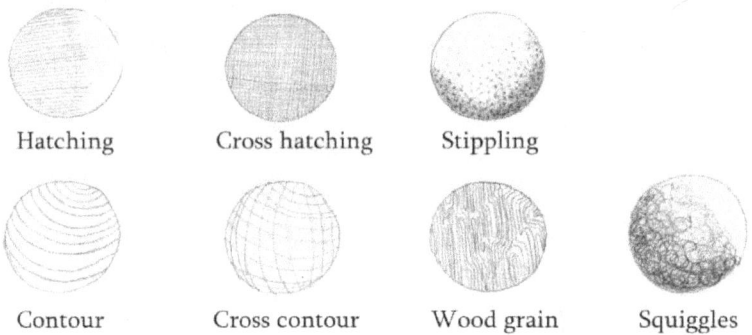

Stippling

This technique is used for finer shading and being more precise in casting shadows.

Contour

This type of shading is often used to help cast shadows from curved surfaces or the more curvy aspects of people and animals.

Cross Contour

This is like cross-hatching.

Wood grain

There will be times you will want to challenge yourself by drawing a wooden surface. This is perfect for that and more abstract shading techniques.

Squiggles

This is used when you need something a little larger than squiggles but not as pronounced as hatching.

Casting your Shadows

The figure is an example of shading. You have to keep in mind about the direction of your light source:

- Which side of the object gets the most light?

- Which side gets the most shade, and where the shadow is cast in relation to the light source?

Things to take note:

1. The darkest part of the shadow is completely hidden from the light.

2. As the cast shadow get further from the object, it gets lighter.

3. The shadow elongates or shortens depending on the light source.

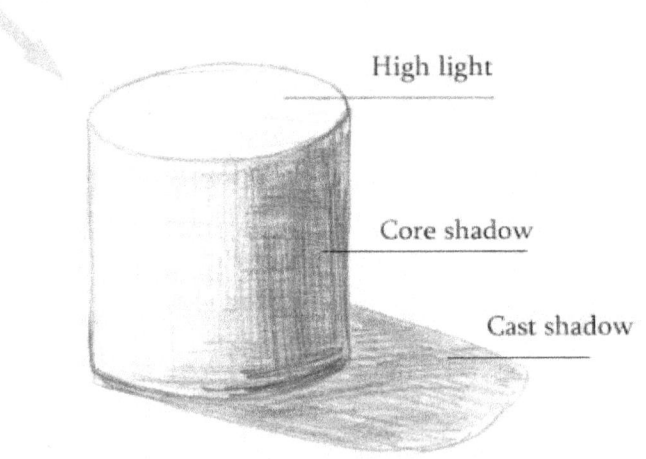

Observation practice

1. Place a stationary object on a piece of white paper.

2. Take a portable light source and shine it on the object.

3. Note, by taking pictures, where the shadow falls and the length of the shadow as you move the light source around the object and where it falls when you move the light closer and further away.

This will give you a great idea on how shadows play a part in creating depth and more detail in your art.

Chapter 4 - Sphere

1. Draw a simple circle.

2. Use the hatching technique to apply the shading in the pattern you see it.

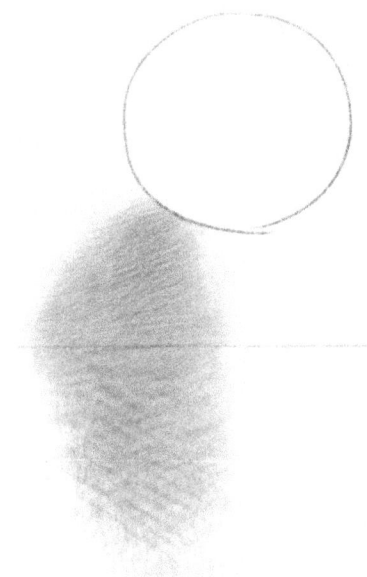

3. Add the contour shading you see in the picture.

4. Use your finger to smooth it out.

Fold you paper the way to see it in the picture above.

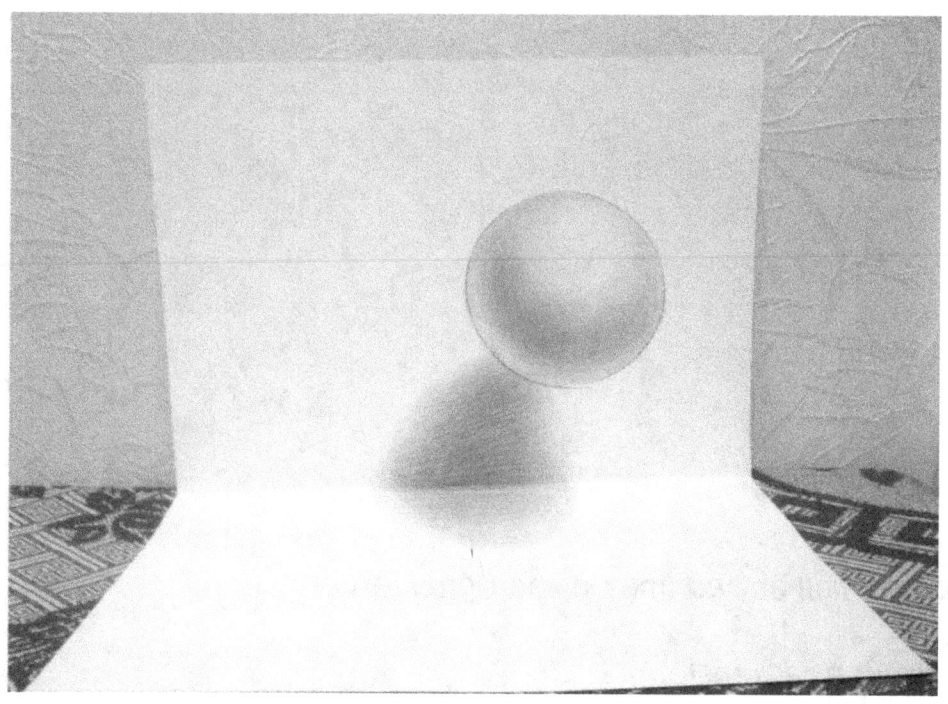

Chapter 5 - The cube

1. Draw the angled "L" you see above.

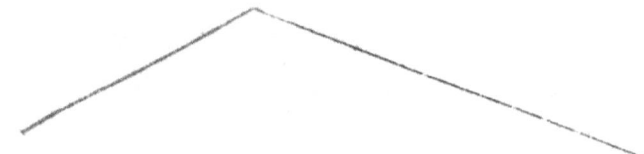

2. Draw the leg of the rectangle you see here.

3. Draw the remaining straight lines as you see them on the left.

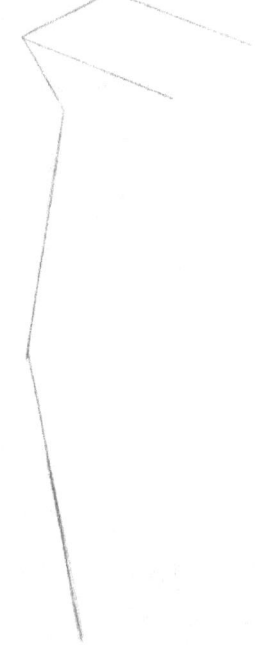

4. Add a small angled line on the right corner.

5. Finish the rectangle.

6. Draw the long, angled line in the middle of the picture.

7. Draw the line angled up from the base.

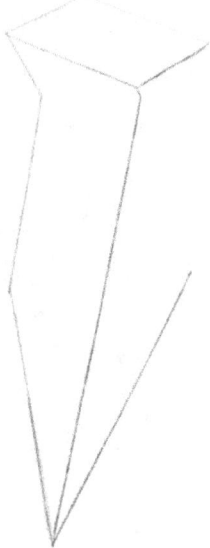

8. Draw the angled lines in the rear of the figure.

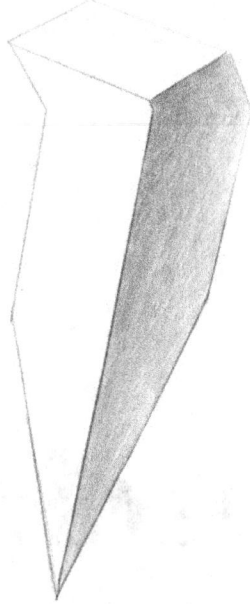

9. Shade the side you see in the picture.

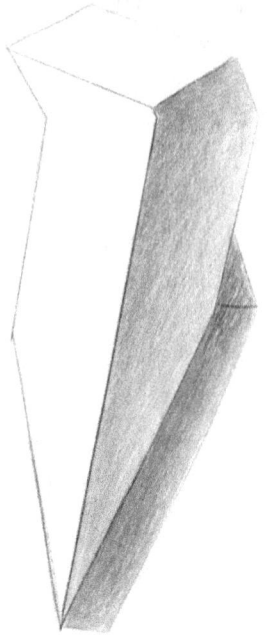

10. Shade it as it is in the picture.

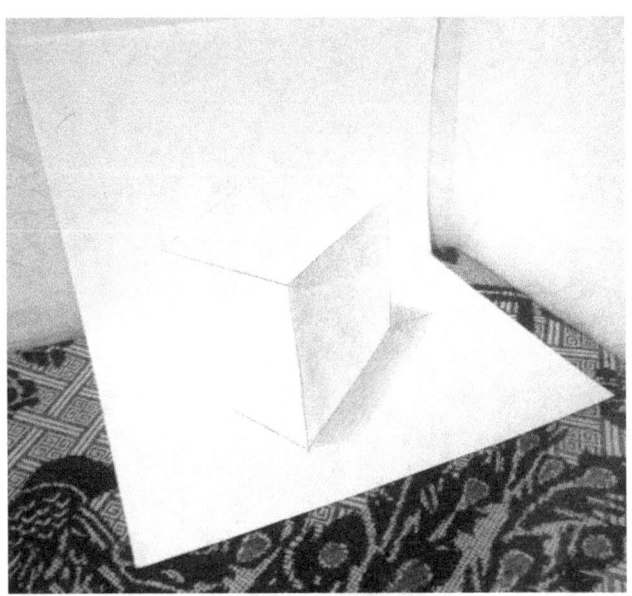

11. Fold the picture as shown to get the effect.

Chapter 6 – Tower

1. Draw the bent lines you see in the picture.

2. Add the angled lines you see in the picture.

3. Draw the straight line in the middle of the tower.

4. Draw the cracked ground.

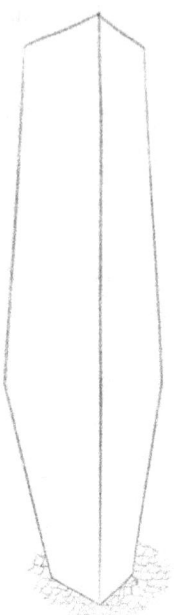

5. Add the shading on the far side.

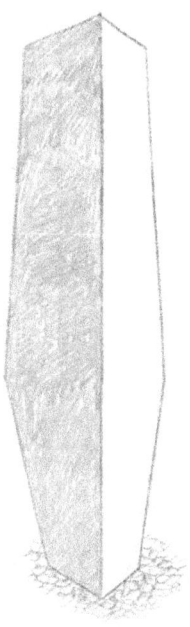

6. Add the rest of the shading.

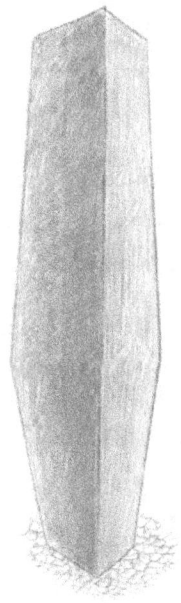

7. Add the shadow of tower at it base.

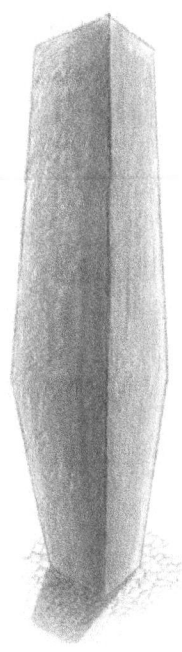

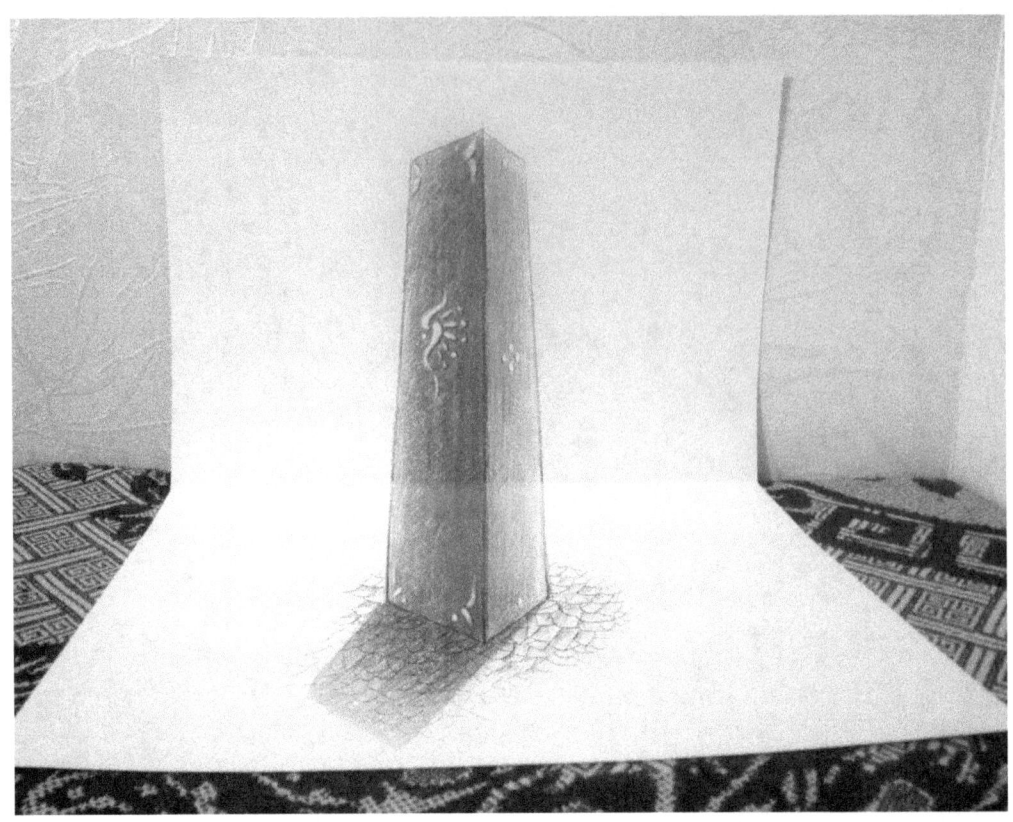

8. Take your eraser and add the accents you see in the picture.

9. Fold the paper like you see it in the picture.

Chapter 7 – Pipe

1. Draw the rectangle.

2. Draw the inside lines.

3. Draw the curves on the left side first.

4. Draw the line coming out of the side.

5. Draw the straight lines coming up from the base pipe.

6. Draw the curve at the base.

7. Draw the circle at the top.

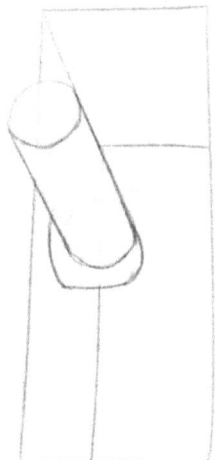

8. Draw the curved line in the picture up from the circle you drew earlier.

9. Draw the curve for the elbow bend.

10. Draw the end of the elbow.

11. Repeat to finish the pipe.

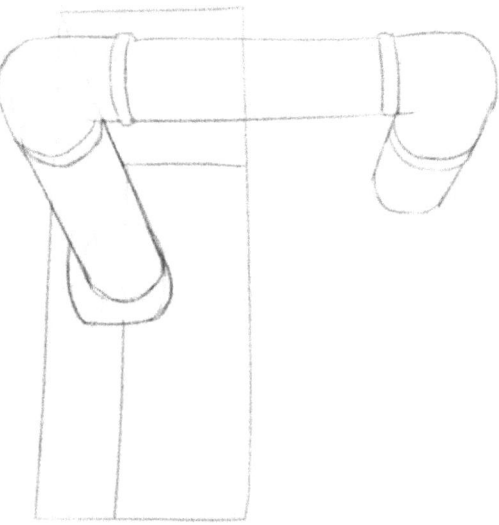

12. Shade the sides you see above.

13. Draw the small circles on the pipe junctions.

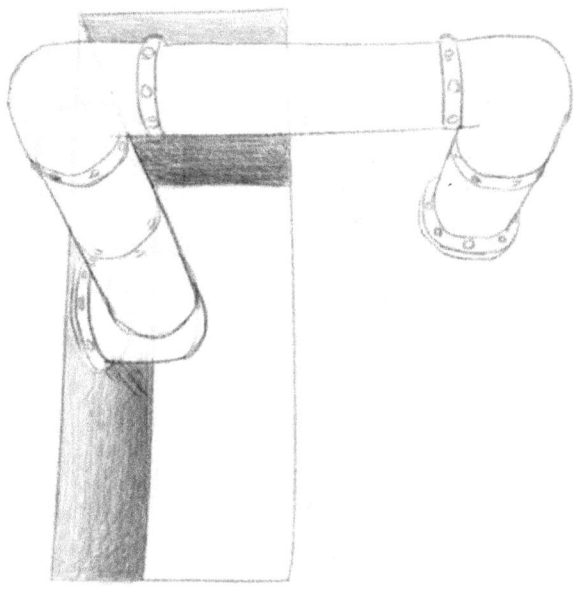

14. Shade the rest of the inside.

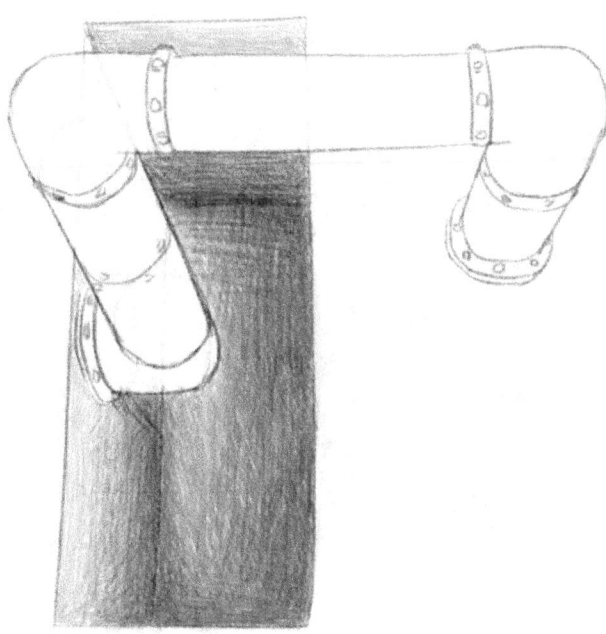

15. Contour hatches the pipes first.

16. Go back and shade the side of the pipe shown.

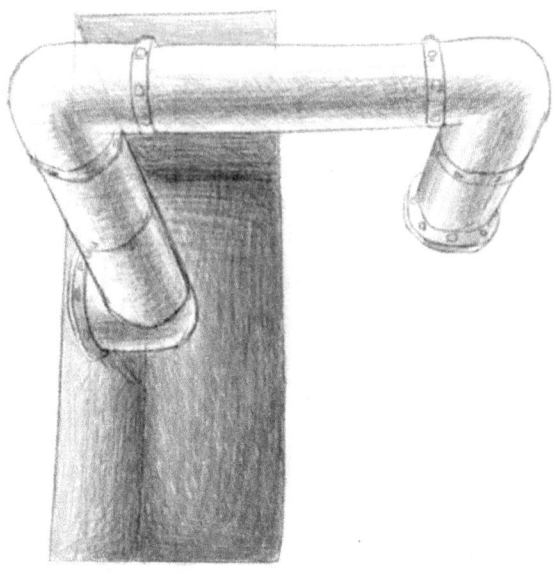

17. Add the shading above.

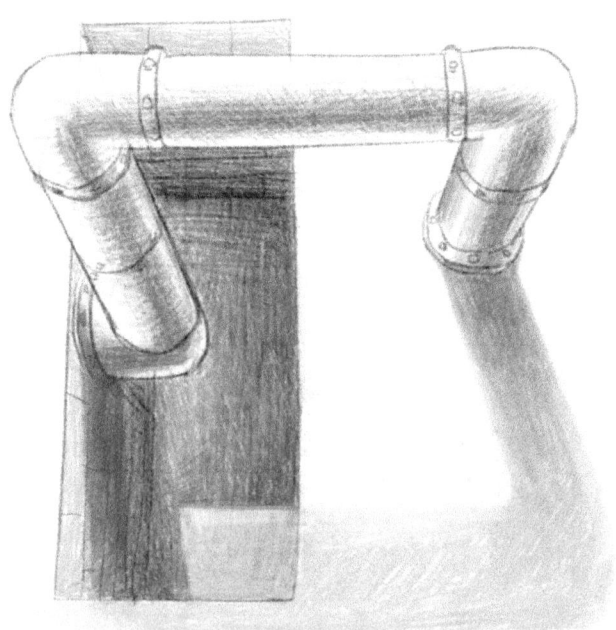

18. Double check the shading here before you the last picture.

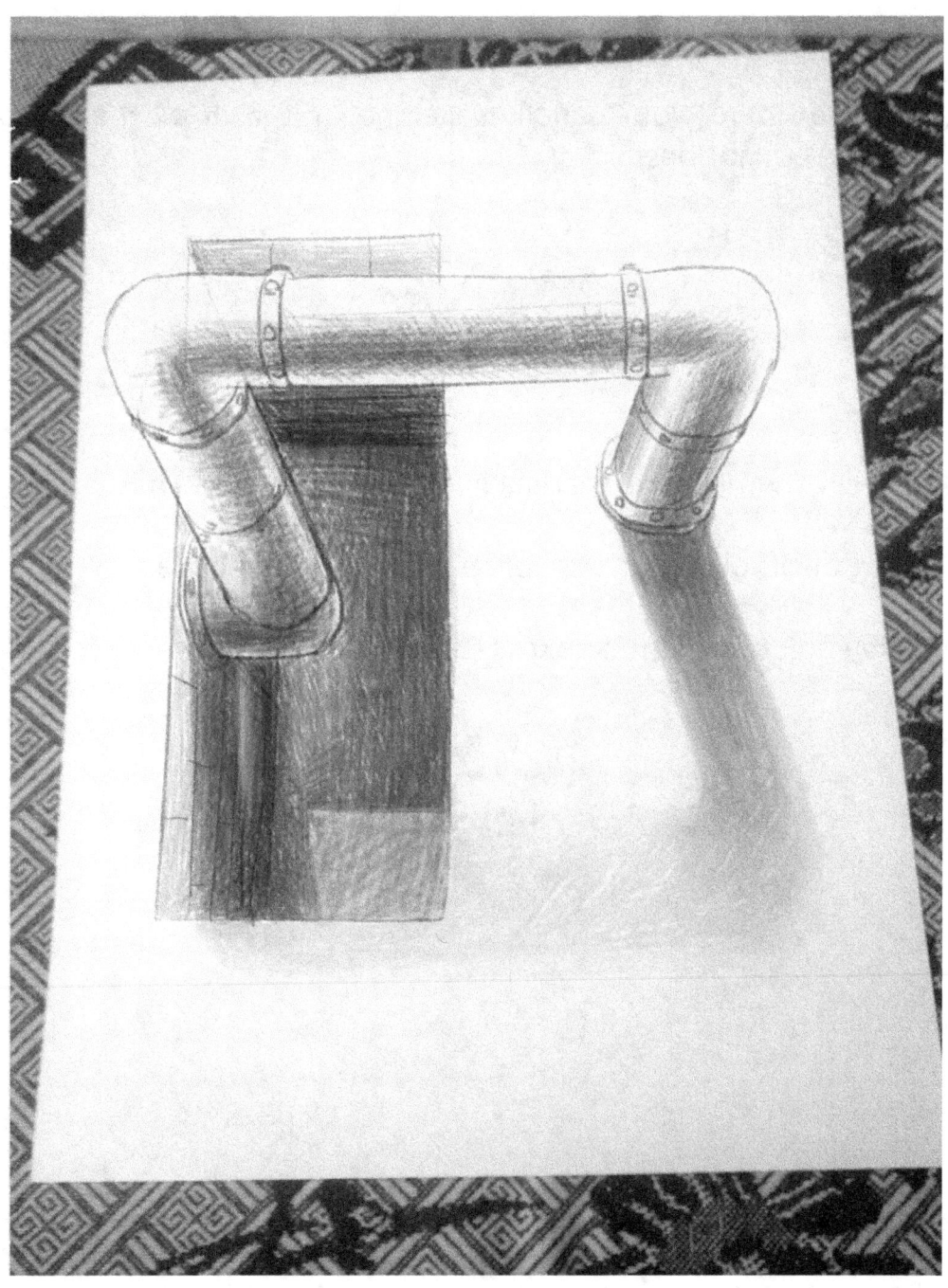

Chapter 8 - Rain Cloud

1. Using the side of your pencil, make the first layer of the cloud by making curved motions.

2. Make another layer of shading marks on top of the first.

3. Repeat until you get the shading in the picture above.

4. Making quick straight strokes, add in the rain drops.

5. Make small check marks for the rain impact.

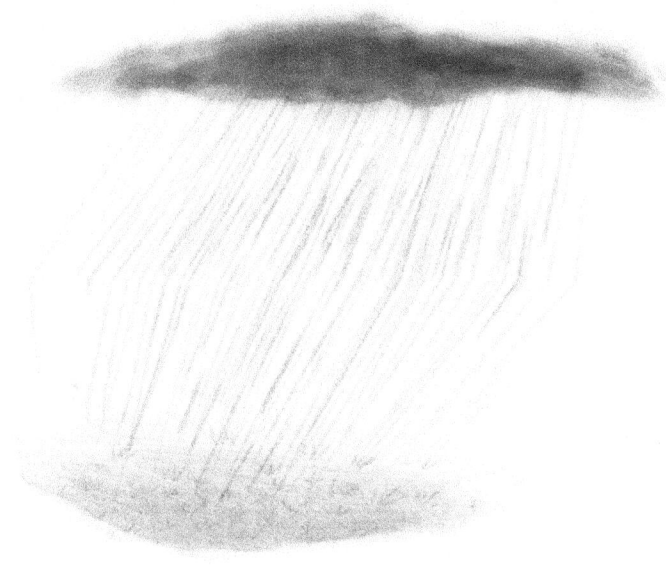

6. Shade in the space under the rain cloud.

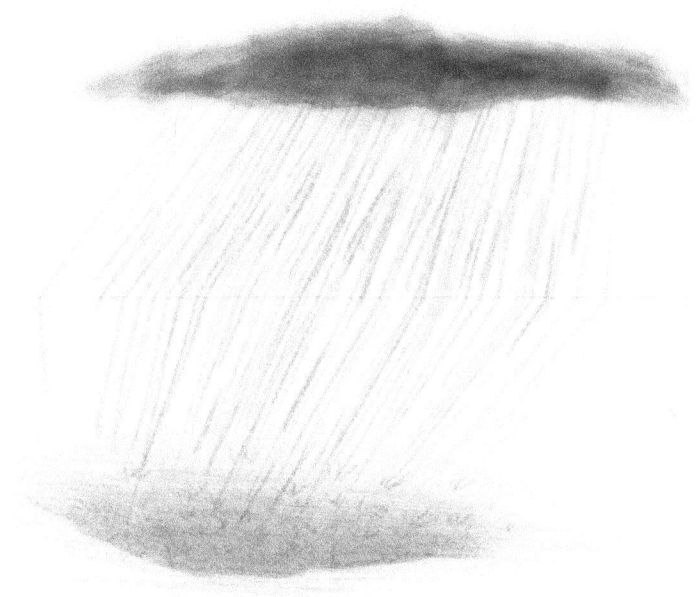

7. Darken in the shading under the cloud.

Fold the paper to the 3D effect.

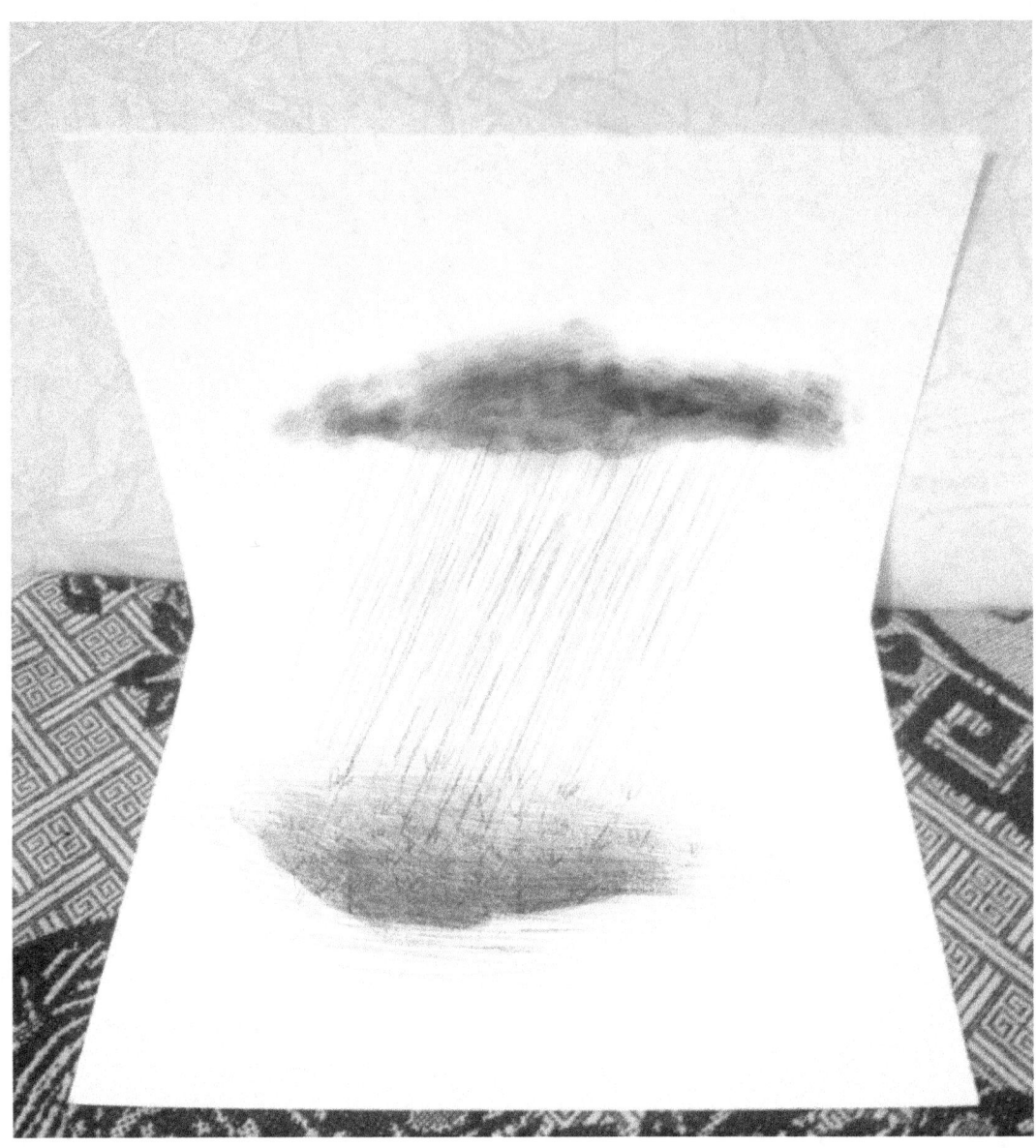

Chapter 9 - Ladder

1. Draw the trapezoid.

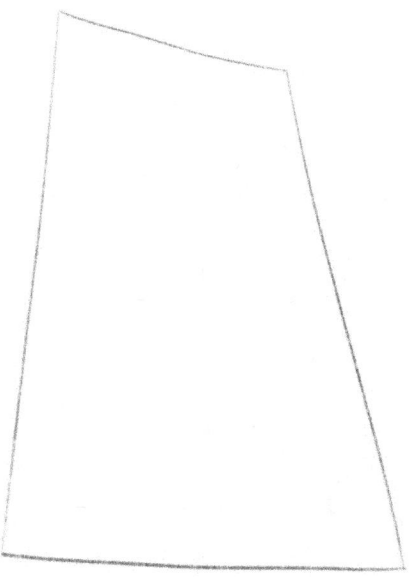

2. Draw the lines going down at an angle.

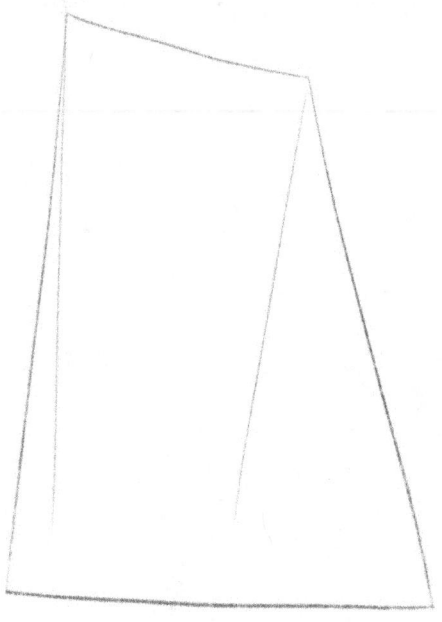

3. Draw the outside lines for the ladder first.

4. Draw the inside lines for the legs.

5. Draw the cross bars.

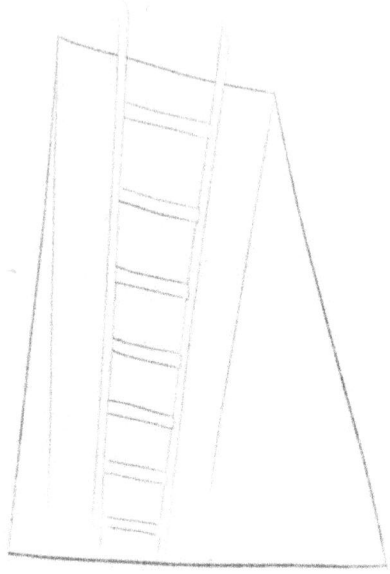

6. Using the side of the pencil, shade the right side of the wall.

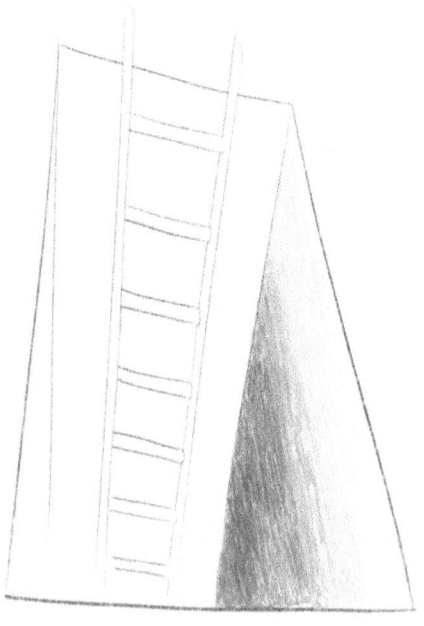

7. Shade the left wall of the picture.

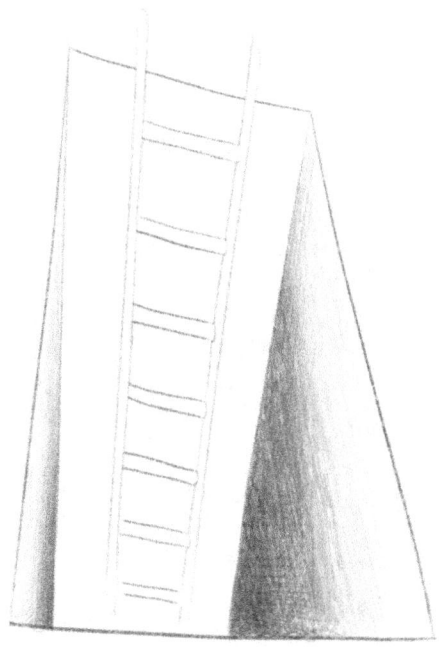

8. Using contour strokes, shade the back wall of the hole.

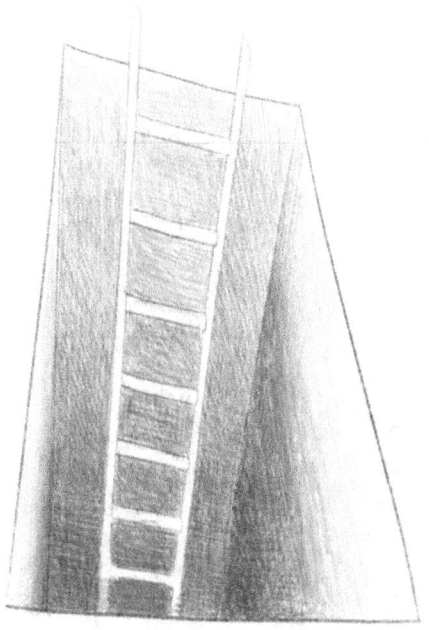

9. Lightly shade the ladder as you see it in the picture.

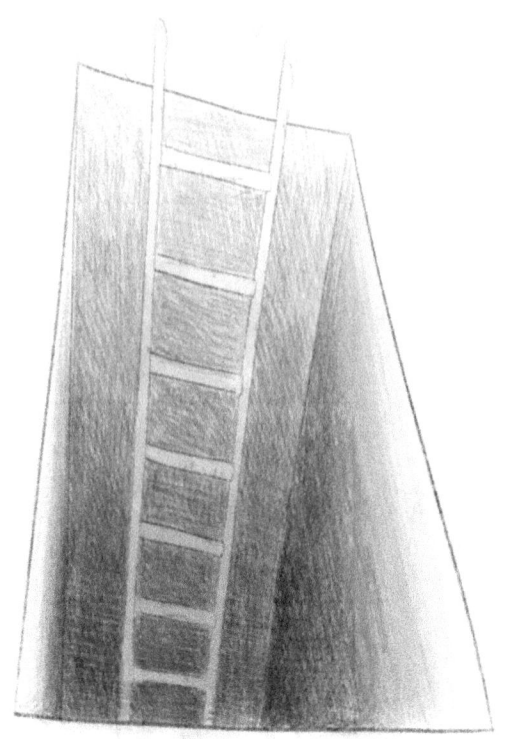

10. Add the lines for the bricks.

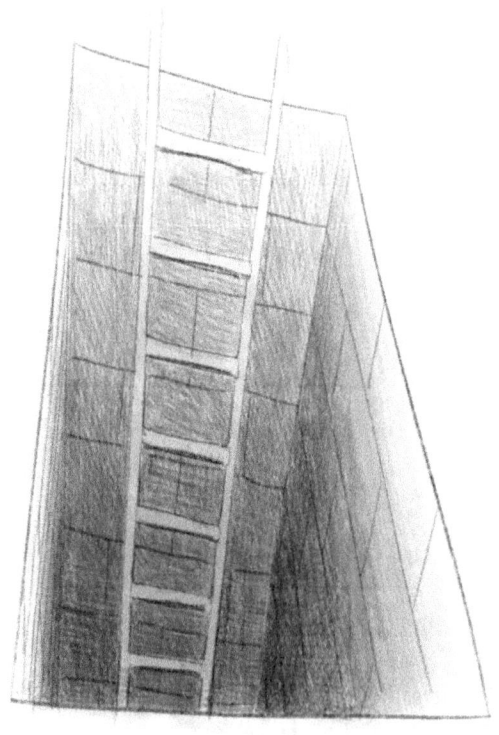

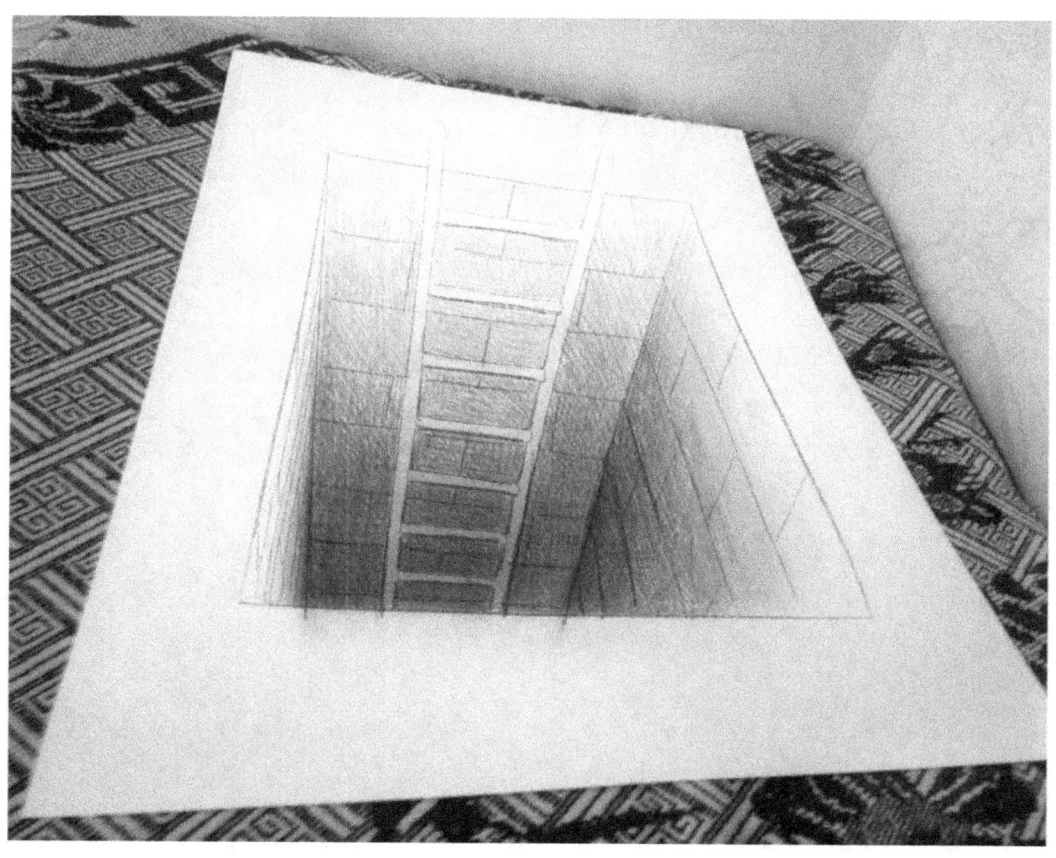

Chapter 10 – Crack

1. Start by drawing a jagged oval.

2. Add the crack lines.

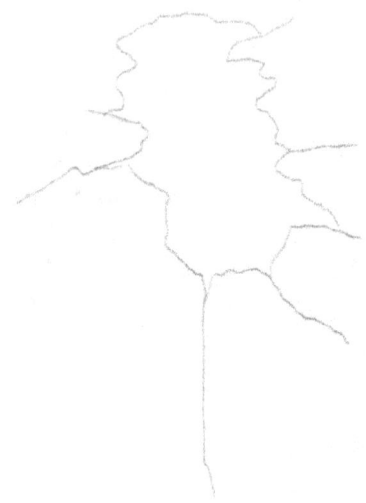

3. Draw the lines down as you see them in the picture.

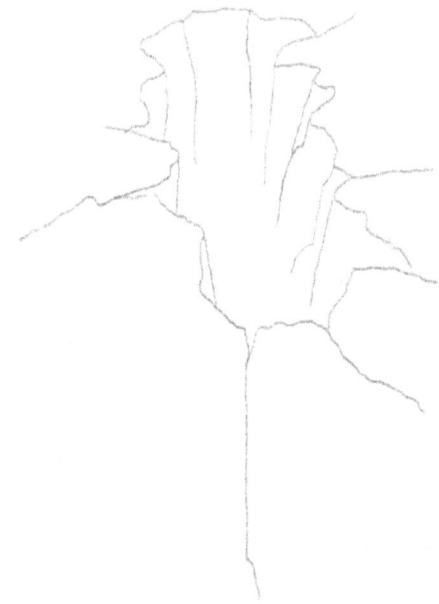

4. Connect the lines at the base of the crack.

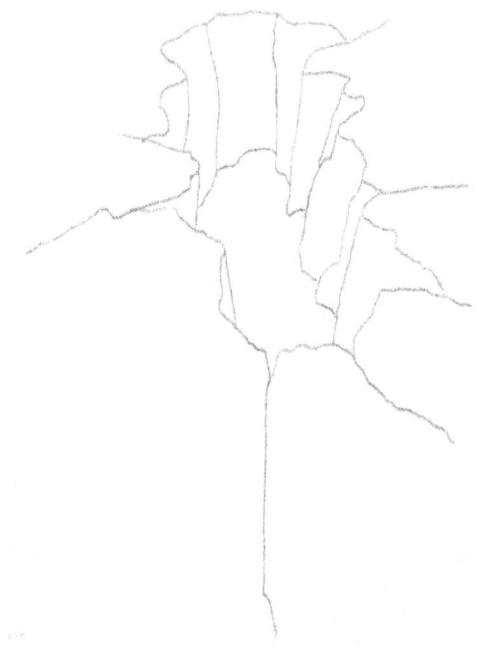

5. Shade the rear of the crack.

6. Bring the shading down on the right side of the crack.

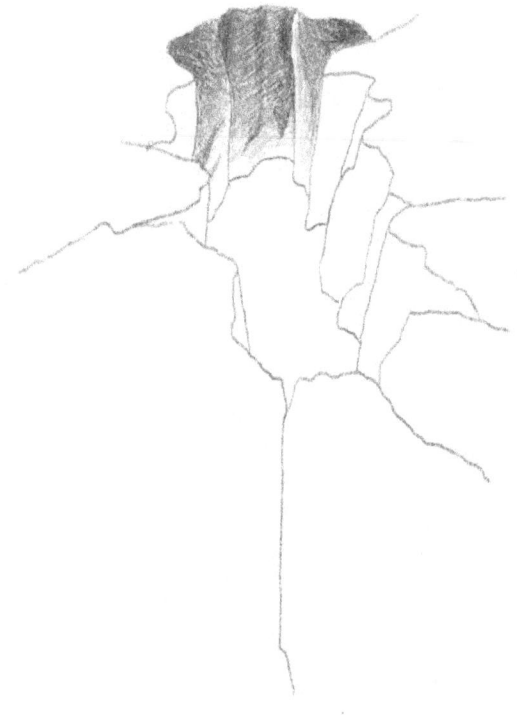

7. Add the light lines in the picture.

8. Add more shading.

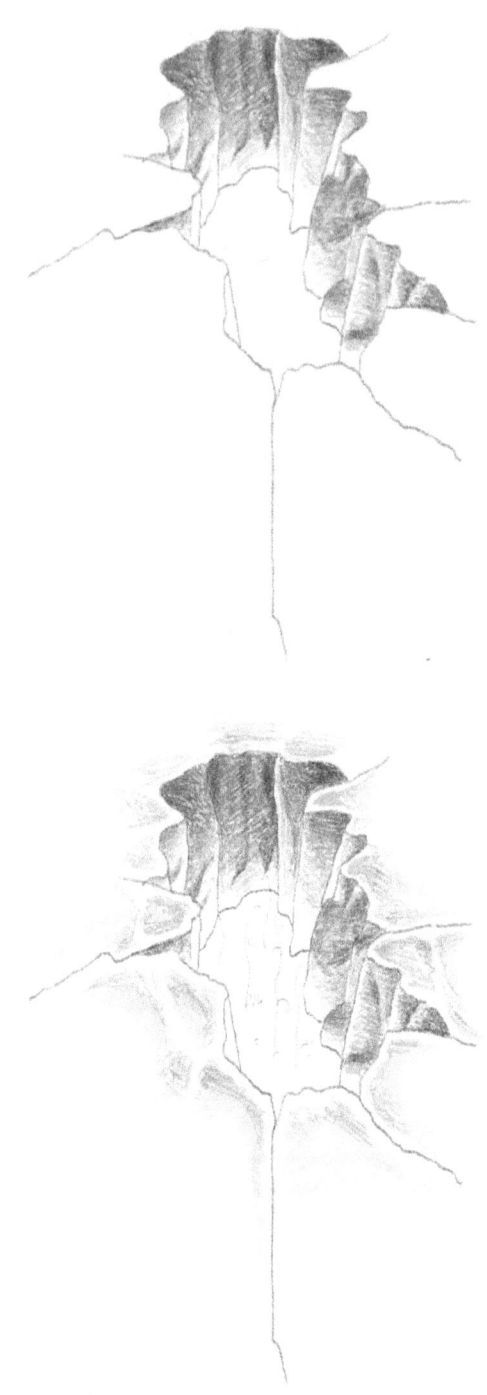

9. Add any missing lines and shading to finish the picture.

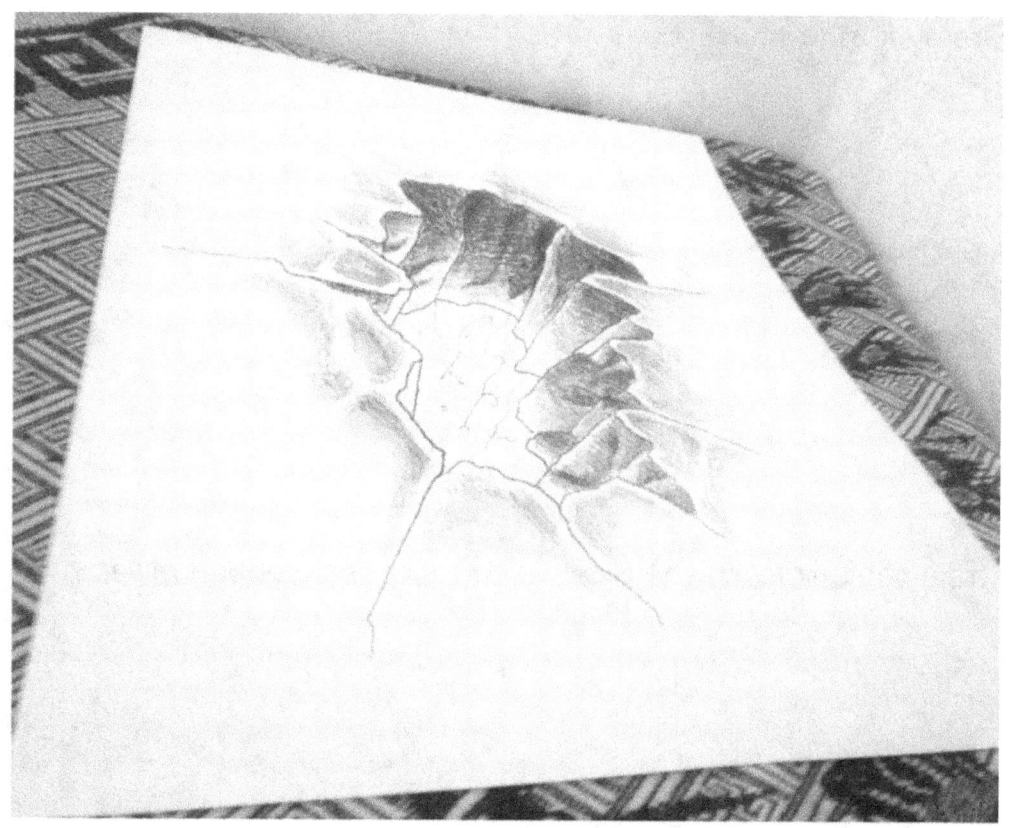

Chapter 11 - Webbed Sphere

1. Draw a circle to start.

2. Draw the circles in the picture to start the webbed effect.

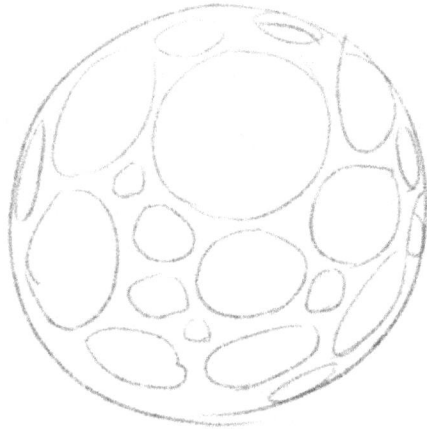

3. Add the extra circles in the picture to add depth to the sphere.

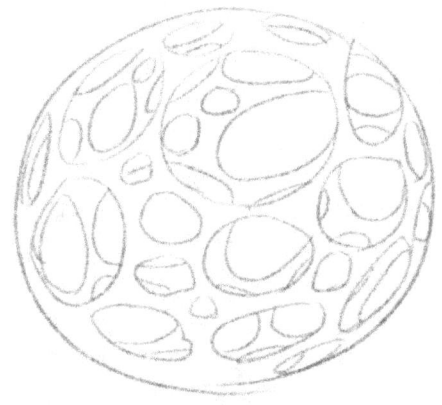

4. Shade the inside of the sphere.

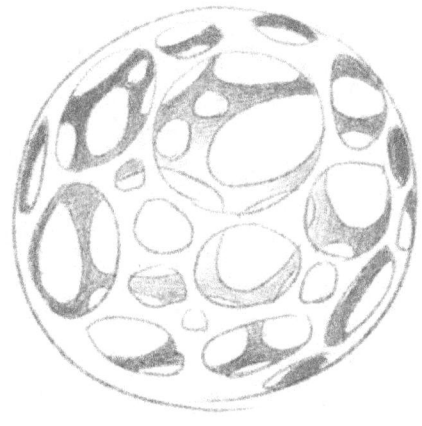

5. Shade the lower half of the sphere.

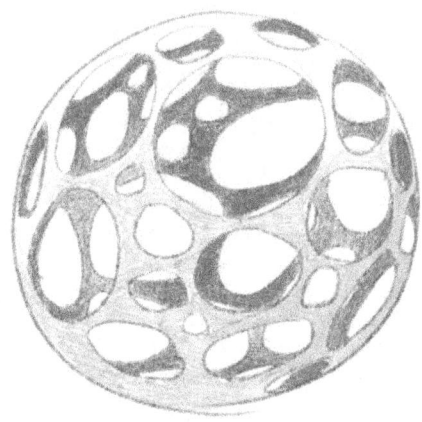

6. Play with the shading toward the base.

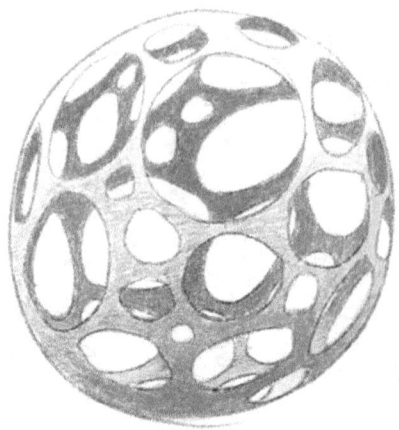

7. Using cross-hatching, add the shadow for the sphere.

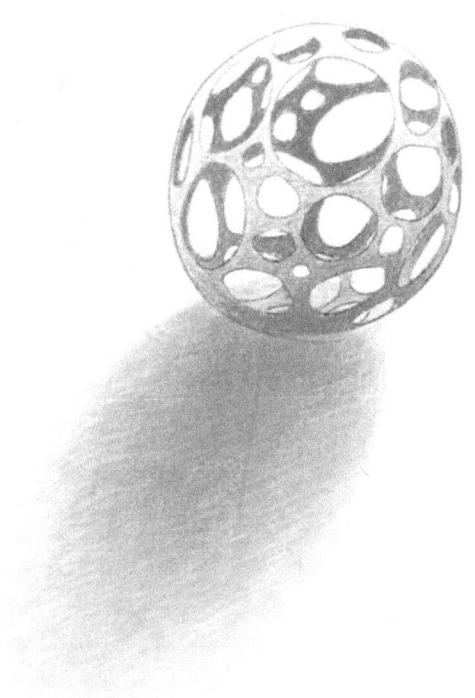

8. Using your eraser, make the shapes in the shadow in the picture.

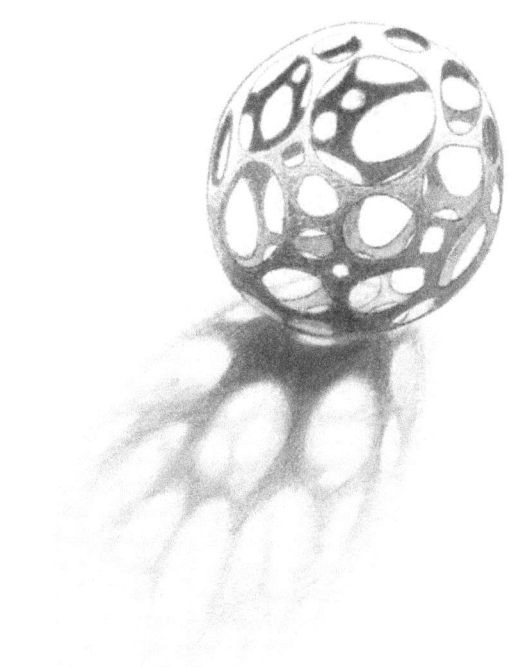

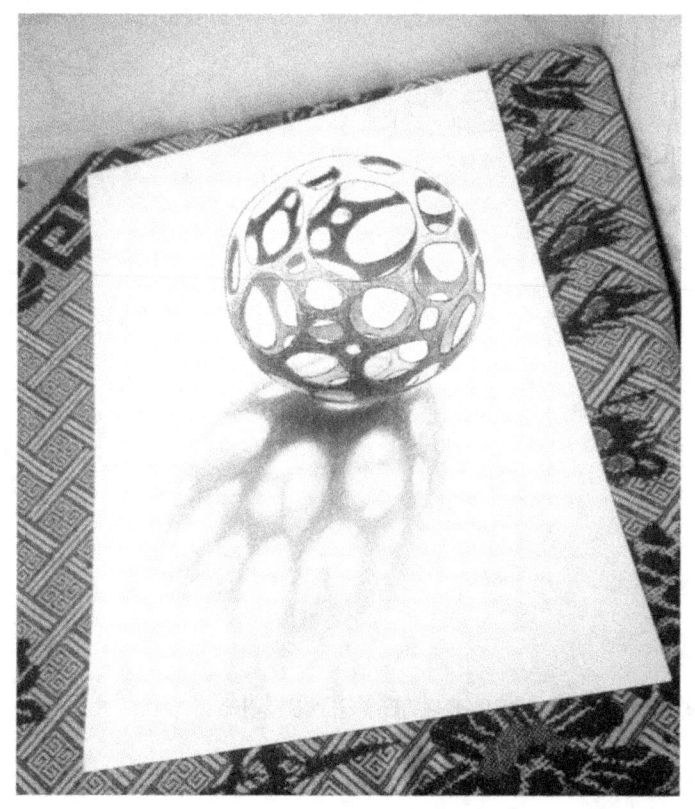

Chapter 12 – Walls

1. Draw the square in the picture above.

2. Add the lines you see above to give it depth.

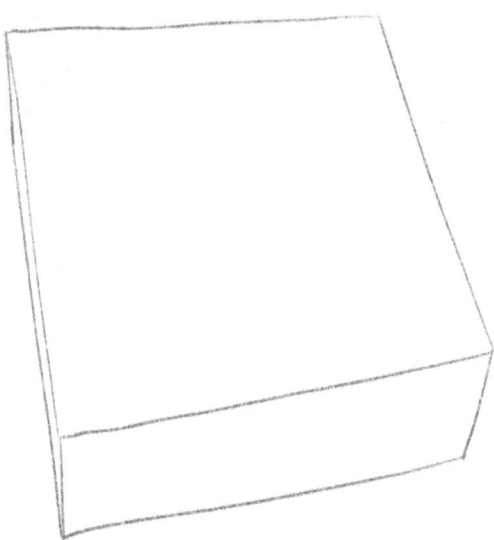

3. Draw the rectangle inside the rectangle.

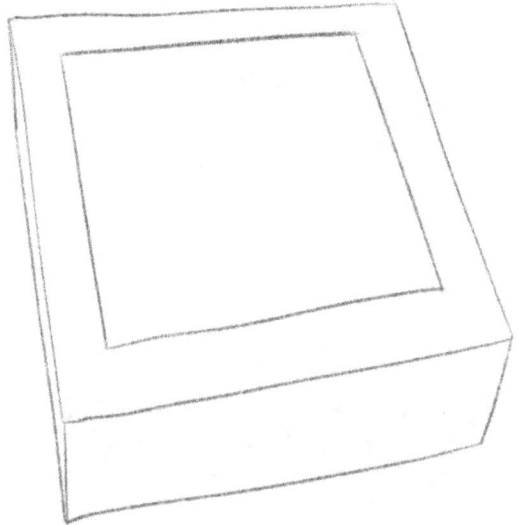

4. Fill in the inside.

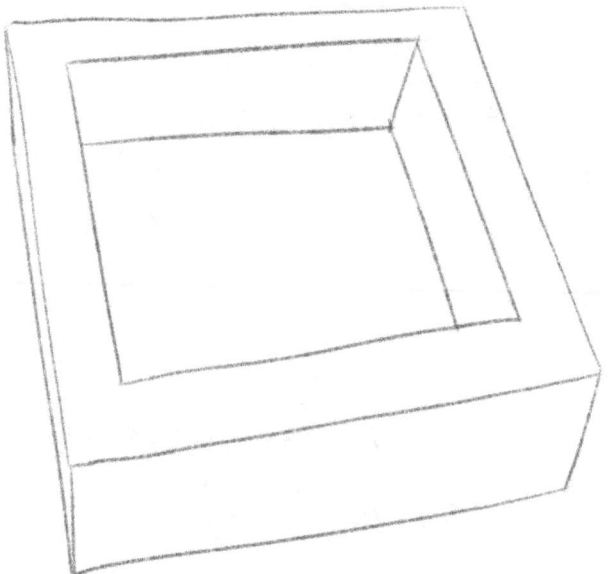

5. Shade the parts shown.

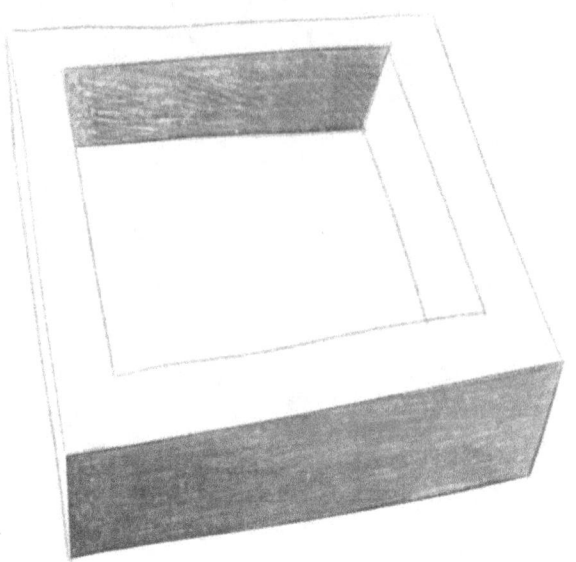

6. Add the other shading as well.

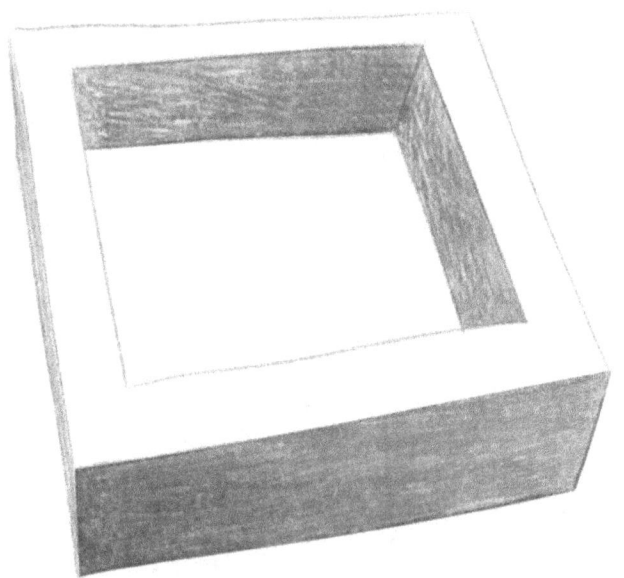

7. Add the rest of the shading.

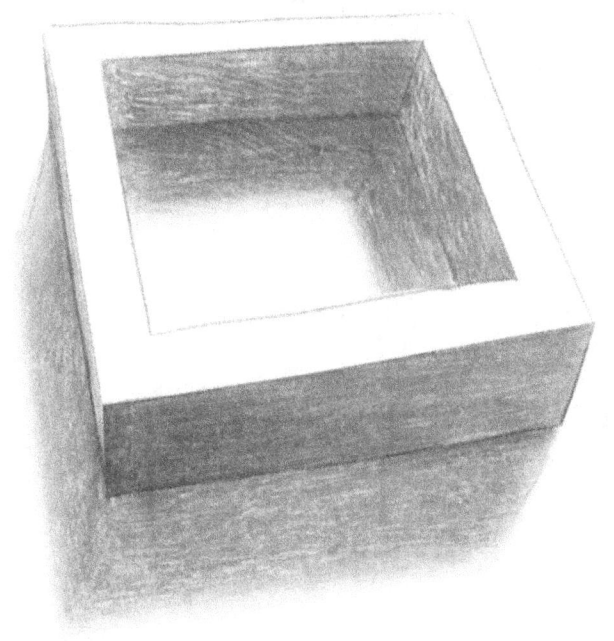

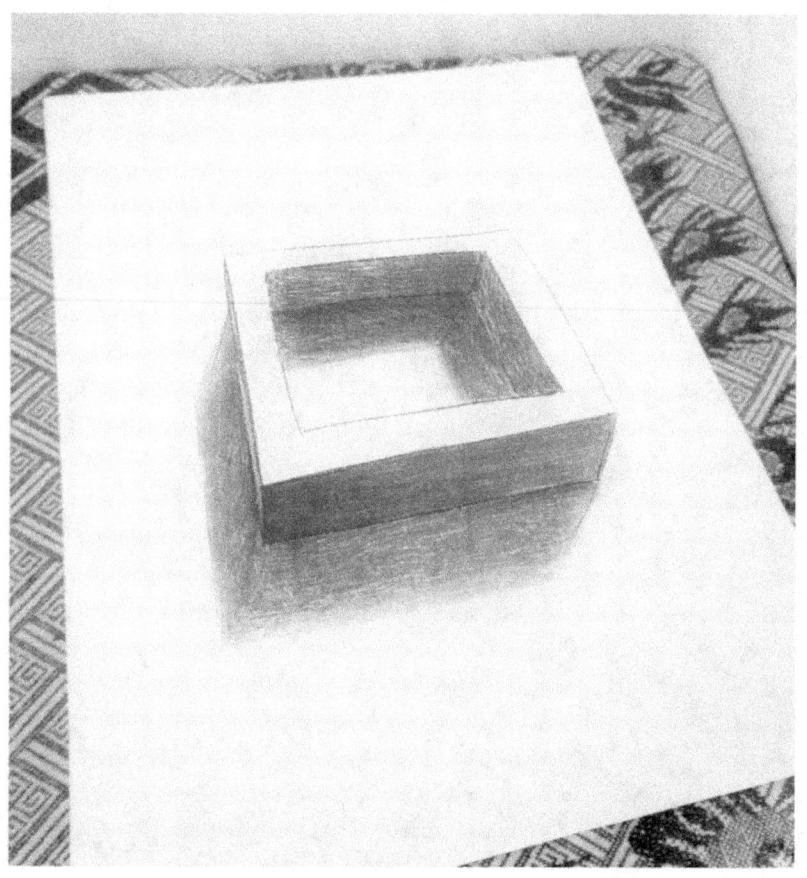

Now You Try

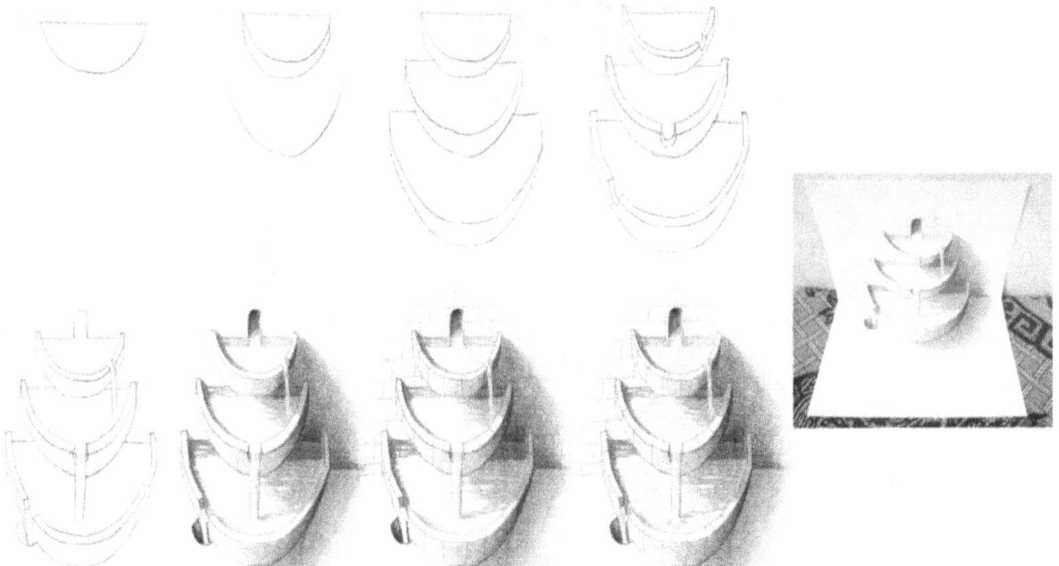

50

Conclusion

Keep challenging yourself. Take pictures of objects you would like to draw in this manner, and then sit down try to draw it. When you're comfortable, you can move one to using water colors, pastels, and other mediums to really make your artwork pop off the page.

If you want to look at others' work, go ahead, but don't do it for comparison. Look at their work and ask yourself how they did it. You know you're excelling when you can figure out how something is done.

I hope this book has helped you start on your new and rewarding hobby.

Thank you!

Thank you for choosing our book, we hope you found it interesting and helpful. If you liked the book, please give us a favor to write your review. We would really appreciate this!
If you would like to have a bonus – **FREE BOOK**, please send the screenshot of your review to this e-mail:
gloria.kemer@gmail.com and we will send you a FREE BOOK in PDF. Hope to see you in our future books and good luck in your drawing experience!

www.ingramcontent.com/pod-product-compliance
Lightning Source LLC
Chambersburg PA
CBHW081122240526
45470CB00019B/2890